S0-AEH-345

CAMINO CIELO

ALSO BY CHRISTOPHER BUCKLEY

POETRY

A SHORT HISTORY OF LIGHT

DARK MATTER

BLUE AUTUMN

BLOSSOMS & BONES:
ON THE LIFE AND WORK OF GEORGIA O'KEEFFE

DUST LIGHT, LEAVES

OTHER LIVES

LAST RITES

NONFICTION

CRUISING STATE:
GROWING UP IN SOUTHERN CALIFORNIA

AS EDITOR

ON THE POETRY OF PHILIP LEVINE:
STRANGER TO NOTHING

(WITH CHRISTOPHER MERRILL)
WHAT WILL SUFFICE:
CONTEMPORARY AMERICAN POETS ON THE ART OF POETRY

CAMINO CIELO

CHRISTOPHER BUCKLEY

For Peter,
with all good wishes
& friendship in poetry
Chris Dec. '96

ORCHISES • *WASHINGTON* • 1997

Copyright © 1997 Christopher Buckley

Library of Congress Cataloging in Publication Data

Buckley, Christopher, 1948-
    Camino cielo / Christopher Buckley.
        p.   cm.
    ISBN 0-914061-58-5 (hardcover : alk. paper) — ISBN 0-914061-59-3 (pbk. : alk. paper)
    I. Title
    PS3552.U339C36   1997
    811'.54—dc 20   96-19976
                                                                              CIP

—ACKNOWLEDGEMENTS—

American Poetry Review	The Presocratic, Surfing, Breathing Cosmology Blues
Black Warrior Review	Late Schoolyard
Cimarron Review	Cruising State
Crazyhorse	Father, 1952; Going Home; Alisos Canyon Contract
Cumberland Poetry Review	Early Morning
The Denver Quarterly	Note to Tomaz Salamun . . .; Jonah
The Hudson Review	Dreaming the Clouds of 1956
New England Review	Art & Science, 1961
The Plum Review	Faith, Prayer After Promotion
Poetry	Sycamore Canyon Nocturne; Eschatology; Equinox
Poet Lore	Washing The Body
The Poetry Miscellany	The Scales
Quarterly West	Old Love; Evening in Cortona; Rain/Light; Camino Cielo
Red Brick Review	All Souls
Santa Barbara Review	There & Then
The Sun	A Prayer at the End of March
Yellow Silk	Singing

COVER: "Coronado Circle" NADYA BROWN

Thanks to: *Pushcart Volume XVIII 1993-94* for a Pushcart Prize for "Sycamore Canyon Nocturne; Greenhouse Review Press for a limited edition broadside of "Sycamore Canyon Nocturne;" *Poems for a Small Planet: Contemporary American Nature Poetry,* in which some of these poems were anthologized; Aureole Press for a limited edition letter press chapbook of Alisos Canyon Contract; the Commonwealth of Pennsylvania Council on the Arts for a grant which supported the writing of some of these poems.

Special thanks to Mark Jarman for revision suggestions for this manuscript; to Gary Young, Jon Veinberg, Gary Soto and Nadya Brown for support and help with these poems.

The publisher and author are grateful to the deans of the College of Arts and Sciences at West Chester University for a CASSDA grant that helped defray the cost of publication.

Orchises Press
P. O. Box 20602
Alexandria, Virginia 22320-1602

G6E4C2A

Out on the mountain-sides, whirling dead
leaves are abroad. Come with me, up here
on the watch-tower . . . Here, at the sea's edge,
we can watch gray clouds torn by winds,
and be sad together
now autumn has returned.

—LI PO

from "Autumn of All Good Things"

My heart of silk
is filled with lights,
with lost bells,
with lilies and bees.
I will go very far,
farther than those hills,
farther than the seas,
close to the stars,
to beg Christ the Lord
to give back the soul I had
of old, when I was a child,
ripened with legends
with a feathered cap
and a wooden sword.

— GARCIA LORCA

from "Ballad of the Little Square"

CONTENTS

I

II

III

I

JONAH

Overcast, close,
done-in with rain—
yet the diaphanous
and chemical rancor
of the air, the effluvium
south of Philadelphia,
like bad luck, will not wash
away.
       Wasn't it you
who once saw palm trees
on a shore, heard a lilt
of canaries to the lee?
Driving past the stacks,
the smoke and run-on gauze—
looking back, looking dimly ahead—
don't you wonder how
you'll ever steer your way
clear of *Childhood,* that story,
that sun-embellished text
from which the least afterthought
of wind tears pages loose
and gives them the blue run
of your heart, brooding
and ubiquitous as clouds?

What forecast for a world
always just over the horizon,
losses now almost immeasurable
against the pastel embarkations

of a sky? Even in dreams
the ocean says nothing
you don't remember.

What will it take to return,
to be blessed with nothing
more weighing your shoulders
than the shadows of afternoon
as you wander speechless
among an apotheosis of light-
charged trees, the white and fiery
mist of leaves you once breathed there
beside the salt breeze and hovering
hours cliff-hung by the unlocked bay?

What prayer could free you,
could place you at the end
of your old lane, overlooking
the Pacific and a channel squall—
the spray like a powder of chalk,
like all those lost markings
on a sidewalk, the loved and airy
loops of every name now dispersed
into years of unmitigated grey?

And wasn't that your name wave-like,
in cursive across the blackboard,
erased then with whitecaps
whipped over the slate-dark swells?
What will you make of it
in these dour and diminished days,
what deliverance from which

vast deep when each hope
you unfold from the vest pockets
of the heart—take out a little at a time
like small notes written to the light—
leaves you still lost and at sea,
rebuked in the dull length
and belly of the east?

FATHER, 1952

                              He must be 30 or 31,
and the brown autumn light is dying
in the tops of jacarandas lining Anacapa Street.
He's just picked me up from school
on the big hill in back of town, and,
riding in our station wagon's wide front seat,
the whole windshield is a field of blue
filled with sea, and a sky bending to meet it
where the earth curves miles out in air . . .
I'm looking up after unlacing my school shoes
and pulling on cowboy boots, black ones
with white and gold lilies blossoming at the tops—
this is not that long ago . . .
                              Forty years,
and it all comes back the day I bend down
to try on a pair of wingtips, and there he is
in his camel hair sport coat and green knit tie . . .
His black and wavy hair blows again in the wind
from the open window of the car—again,
we're taking the curves above the Mission,
the limestone walls and pepper trees aflame
along the road, and in that last blindness of sun,
the mackerel clouds, the clusters of pepper pods
burn red as the bell-tower domes . . . .
I'm staring into the light spread thick as sawdust
across the windshield. With his college ring
he's tapping out a tune on the steering wheel,
stubbing a Philip Morris. Now he's whistling,
it's 4:30, and the daylight behind us is going

violet on the mountain range. I'm content
in my boots, standing on the green vinyl seat
to see above the dash—below, a harbor mist
rolls in beneath the yellow nettle of stars,
the Xs of seagulls' wings marking their places
as they drift slowly before the dark. I'm looking left,
into the purple sky—we're coasting down
a last silent hill. Nothing, I think, has happened
in our lives—he's happy—this is not that long ago . . . .

ESCHATOLOGY

Stepping off the sun-bright bus
onto that hilltop and the school,
holding my cap, brown sack
of cookies and fruit, surf sounds
in windy eucalyptus fading as we were
delivered to class, I wore a beaten expression
I'd recognize years later in films
on the faces of those sentenced to life
in prison, the factories, or sent to war.
What was my complaint so early on—
that the miserable lunches were cold,
that the boys' hair was bobby-pinned in place
before we were herded to Benediction
for 40 days during Lent, that the omniscient
chalk dust in the rooms seemed more
a byproduct of the good Sisters hearts
than our attempts at knowledge or at grace?
Yes, all of that, but more likely, it was general,
indistinct as that atmosphere of fire and death
from which the angel with the flaming sword
drove our wild and venial hearts out
of chapel chastened and denied.
Still, it was vague as that fog climbing
each morning blindly from the sea,
and on clearer days after class
I became the confidant of clouds
and kept a place in my mind to go
with them and know air and light alone
as I breathed in that tree top

coveting the abandonment of birds.
Perhaps it was only that we were governed
by edicts of comportment and commands
stressed slowly from the severe mouths
of beings so removed from the world
that even their concern for themselves was less
than the chill mists which filled the foothills,
the shallow places where some sun
seeped rarely through.
                  A little reason
and kindness were reward for regiment,
for narrow conformation to the subtle
requests of power. Each day it seemed possible
that this might be endless, or that our lives,
temporal or otherwise, might not; each day
we were made to hand over our wills
in silence like notes passed during class.
What fulfillment could there have been
terrifying such easily astonished souls
away from our best learned instincts
toward disobedience and desire for a world
which lurked, rich and free as light
just beyond the sea-colored acacia
and monkey puzzle trees? Or beyond
the high wrought-iron gate, where
at each day's end, two or three stood—
black sentinels watching us turn away past
banana palms and flowering pittosporum—
stale and silent, sure they alone held
the dark knowledge of every final thing.

GOING HOME

They're altogether otherworldly now . . .
—ROBERT LOWELL

Grandmother, 100 now, in a home
in a small town south of Columbus,
a town from which she's never moved,
sees it only that way now—her body tied
in the weakest manner to the mind,
a bird fluttering all day about the blue,
returning at dark to nest . . .
                                        Each day
the roads that once were dirt
are dust again, spun up
on the air in slowed amber veils
and swirls as cars stutter along
and the evening light breaks down.
Or she sees the first combine chafing through
the neighbor's field of alfalfa, wild flowers
and flax, her son in coveralls still running
after in the rows . . .
                                Then the streets
were paved, then the shoe factory
was surely a job as good as any;
everyone worked, and on Sundays,
drove a dust grey Hudson out
the country roads, the attendants
at filling stations in uniforms and ties;
at home, everything staying fresh in the Norge.

18

Nothing to it. Nothing more complicated
than the light retreating across the west
field at dusk as grandfather in the tiny kitchen
sliced Swiss cheese for his Saltines, while
on his lap, I peered through a hole
to where the dot of sun was slipping
down beyond the roofs . . .
                              After dinner,
he'd take me out for a "drive," to a roadhouse
where he could get a glass of beer,
and be known for an hour among friends,
where I stood on a red plastic stool top,
mindful of my manners with a 7-Up.

Jesus. What world was that?
Hard to imagine now that we were ever
the mild citizens of that state.
Anymore, it's at best some light
hovering in a mind which is also all but lost,
all but dust again . . .
                              And what world is this—
my father gone, taken suddenly and as unaware
as anyone will ever be by a virus virtually unknown?
How many layers can be peeled back
and still find us saying, this life like no other?
Yet where they are, I hear you can turn back
the light to when you were all eagerness
and health, where whatever it was that sang
like a blue charged breath of light through your cells
becomes you, and carries you on . . .
                              And now,
after all this time, my grandfather is opening

the screen door again, stepping out on that
small cement front porch—my father's coming
home from school, whistling something,
walking down their wide dusty lane
where the autumnal half-bare trees that line Ohio
go red and gold at the wind's thin edge,
and in the late afternoon sun flare
forever, glorious as angels' wings . . .

WASHING THE BODY

Begin with vinegar—white flame to burn the unessential
salts away and carry off Death's cheap aftershave, though
a low fog hovers in the empty railway station where

he still sits in his black conductor's coat and cap, smoking a pipe
behind the smudged office window, the arrivals and maple scent
of tobacco faintly on the air. And who cares what you call it—

bundle of old reeds, abraded light, fabric with every vignette un-
threaded from the coarse weave and warp of time . . . call it worry
gone wrong, the sallow years stacked like sidecars and left to rust.

Erase the creases and grease of hope, scour the elbows, the lines
going nowhere now across the hands, those pathetic flowers . . .
The forehead then, the grids of cities still going up there in smoke,

a lost army trailing over the smoldering hills—rinse it down, even
to the planks worn grey as rain. Last blood drops in the water
bucket, six red notes, wireless thinning sound, spread out like

a sunset might above a horizon where the violin-necked geese
call piteously in retreat, their loose curve always shaping that
abstract direction of remorse . . . Someone steps out on the porch

for a smoke, looks off there as if distance came to something—
dull glimmer of a photo, or a pack of Luckys crushed and thrown
into the street? Is it Martha or Valeska who will come and,

breathing on the window glass, round out a bare place
with her fingers against the cold to feel absolutely what is left,
and look into that circled sky, yellow as a wreath of old thorns—

Ohio that long ago, who's to say what lights could ever again
come on over a town so long gone and small with living?
When she touches the black nest of stitches, the tiny galaxy

edged below the heart, she'll then walk to the window and
open it for air, and the dark that's been gathering all day under
leaves and roots, a dark that, by then, will have already risen

to fill the sky, will rush in blowing every tall taper out—
fingernails, flanks, feet, even the waxy shoulders turning
quickly then white and clear—back to the body of stars.

EQUINOX

Wine-sap aura and atmosphere,
pale as if flour had been sifted
over the horizon's long rope
as it cinches up the day and leaves us,
leads us to that last ash or amber space
between the boughs that a thousand starlings fill
like a shower of black stars, reiterating
their harsh sense of the dark, which is only
the distant shattering of waves.

                                     But first
there was the hazy fusion of afternoon
and all the suspended particulate of the past—
chaff and luster, a boy breathing
in the ease and comfort of a loneliness
sung back vaguely from the sea,
salt sting and undertow, the surf-like surging
of his blood across the concourse of days—
all the assemblies of light extending
the spindrift parameters of his arms
where he's seen the floating clouds stall
with their tin-foil shimmer and reserve,
as if Plato's souls were still hovering,
wondering whether to come down.

Now a wind swims through redwoods
and the ridge's alphabet of pines leans high
and away—to Peru it's easy to say, where,
in a book once, he saw someone equally in mists,
mountainside or plateau, playing a flute beside

mild animals—that slight tremolo the wind
knows in its grey way around the heart,
that the grasses know among the stones—
the sky open to everything on its own
thin exhalation.
              This is the sky I know.
Coal-white geranium of sun, distance clearing
and almost colorless, blood smear across glass,
the world powder-blue and full of the silent
desire of air.
              4:30 and a little yard-fire smoke
recommends a moon, the ionic clouds sleepless
again with their old, gilt-edged verisimilitude—
that we should never die, that finally there's no secret
in all the starlight that has yet to reach us.

LATE SCHOOLYARD

Stand here, let the light summer air sift
to light long enough and all you've done
turns back in time, which is everything
for a while—the few clouds are flash cards
above a palimpsest of dust, scrawl of fog swallowing
the paleolithic and indifferent rocks, the oceanic musk
of olive trees still drifting for the sea . . . .

Here and there only the exception of a tree—
otherwise, there you are again on your knees.
No, not praying as you should have then
for the pollen of that sun to sing more slowly down
that glassy bequest of sky, not praising your breath
or legs, neither of which wore out across the playing field
or fell short against the ground winds and burning tides of grass.
No, your heart's floating there, stalled, unconscious
as any cloud, dove-white and momentarily free
of rain, but brooding nonetheless as you knuckle down
and aim your half-pint shooter along a twist of acacia root
for a spot where it will escape the line of fire from a boy,
you'll end up knowing 40 years into the unforeseeable
future, which is always shuffling there, foot to foot,
just off-stage in the wind-hooked stanzas of afternoon
that sift perpetually down the blooming eucalyptus boughs,
undetected as time . . .
                              So there you are,
corporal of the powdered kingdoms of dirt
ground down by a hundred tennis shoes and rising
into the air as his cat's-eye careens off a shard of bark

and picks your marble out, nicks it ever so slightly
in the silence there, that the last angel leaving his duties
for the day, stops in his robe of leaf mist and smoke
and listens for an instant, but turns away thinking
it was only the mirrors hauled up behind the first stars,
or the gearing of crystal spheres as the last bell rings
across the hills.
                    No witnesses, and you disclaim the hit, defy
the breathless click of glass on stone, that first clear-cut
indication of loss, that invisible ink on your hands
as you grab up your blue-white agate and race
for all the world down the asphalt drive toward home—
sneakers leaving their trail of dust, the spikes
of aloe vera flaming coal-red against the sandstone wall,
and over your shoulders the waves of shade
from the high line of trees repeating
the destined and dark shape of wings.

THERE & THEN

Though there's no going back,
it happens all the time—sleep or day-dreams,
and I'm on the corner of State and Micheltorena,
noon on a Saturday, the wide sidewalks shimmering
with mica, Simonized Chryslers and Oldsmobiles, women
with coral or ivory shopping bags sauntering in and out of I. Magnin,
Lou Rose, as I wait for Fowler, Cooney, and Schneider, the station wagons
that will let them out and leave us on our own in all the world we know, seaside
among white stucco and red tile roofs, a little principality of blue air and sun where
someone with a dollar in change is free. Flipping 50¢ pieces, we strut with confidence
into Woolworth's for M&Ms weighed-out by the pound and then head down to the California
Theater on Canon Perdido, the last place where, still under 12, you get in for 15¢. No loges,
a descending center aisle, and we sit in the cave-like glow, in 1959 content to know almost
nothing about our lives or what we're about to see despite a newsreel and our first year
of Social Studies. We're happy, our hightop sneakers squeaking on the sticky floor,
the freight of sugar so thoroughly embalming our veins that we're fairly oblivious
to whatever Robert Mitchum and Yvonne De Carlo, Mel Ferrer and Joan Fontaine
are up to. We're supposed to be at the Arlington for cartoons, Audie Murphy
and John Wayne, World War II again, where one dollar leaves us barely
enough for JuJy Fruits or Junior Mints. So we opt for black & white,
the burning silver profiles when someone's kissed. We can't tell
Film Noir from Adult Romance, but guess what we see goes on
somewhere in the world, though no one we know drinks
martinis, flies to Mexico or Singapore. Four hours with
previews and intermission—we exit walking slowly
up the ramp in the building's shade before
stepping out, almost blinded by the slant
of winter light sharp as tin foil
as we shield our eyes.

Next year, it's 50¢ for everyone,

and we'll go there only one more time

for *Alexander The Great* starring Richard Burton,

something we think we'll understand—the spectacle and bloody technicolor war.

And though Alexander dies reasonably young at 32, that point in time floats out

further than the ancient past. The rainbow of neon tubes hum on, the marquee

fizzes and pops in the 5:00 dusk as I'm the last one to be picked up. When the doors

close for good, I'll remember little about that battle for the civilized world raging

all afternoon—I'll recall instead the face of Kim Novak, tragic and blond in a love

scene as Kirk Douglas walked out on her a year or so before, and there and then

think I know the complete depth and extent of loss, coming soon, out of the dark.

RAIN/LIGHT

Dimensionless
blotter, daylight
like white ink soaked
away—take the sinking
east and say this
is what it's come to—
cyanic bruise
sutured
at the ocean's edge,
sky thick as your
palm print against
the double glazed
window glass . . .

The honey locust
and heavy brambled green
gone grey, slate, stale
as clouds fallen and risen
from the torpor of the lawns.
Gun barrel border
of the seaboard breaking up
for one articulated strand
of sun to rust
along the rose canes
and thinly sound
their thorny stops.

Against the rheumatic
wall you cast

the scenic flourish
of the West—
purple crepe
of the hibiscus flowers,
unwound and wild
on the baranca's ledge, bled
sunward by ground swirls
below the ice plant's
blooms—saffron, rose,
and ice-white—starring
the palisades, like a sky
about to rise
where the calm
pronouncements of air
flourish in the aquatic
limbs of eucalyptus . . .

Sunset filters the air, empty
sound of rain ending
collecting on the ground—
the ghost ship
silhouette of a robin
atop the roof
with a last song
for the coral sea lanes
of the sun . . .

Fifteen billion years,
blue out of
the three-degree dark,
light has misted down
to be here, never

catching up with its own

dispatch and drive.

Each of us,

no more resourceful

than stars, touched

with the abandoned

thought of home . . .

II

ALL SOULS

Stars clear overhead and shot bright
as water from a hose, last ones burning
in needles of flame as long ago as August—
now we needn't hold our breath except
against the cold arriving in its increments
from the vacant angle of space.

Tonight we'll pull our collars up looking
to the sleepless clouds to make our case
for everlasting in their silver undercoats
and current spanning the light-split edge
of sky—this life, some life perhaps to come . . .

Again it is time to offer our estimations
under an early persimmon moon and sit out
long enough to see it etch the ivy's edges
as they climb the drainspout toward another
unknowable space.
              Yesterday we praised
the bay laurel and lindens, daylight's ambered
twigs holding where mockers and finches
proclaimed their quick devotion to the sweet
concourse this side of everything, and we felt
sustained, reassured, knowing no love more
immeasurably given out.
              That was the world—
full for a while of an old silence recast
from an evening's purple woods or dust-
colored plains of pampas grass, a slow

and resonant spell, similar to harp strings splicing
the atmosphere after all the music has stopped
and you again are one of the last to leave your seat
as the auditorium dims . . .

                    The cool bronzed
breathing of the leaves, a last fusion of sun
in coral or violet after-tones over industrial roofs,
the slack and discursive fields . . .

                      The grey sorrow
we always think is coming is coming—thumbprint
of winter and all we've let the air become . . .
Though here, just after 4:00 and the first wind rise,
the horizon burns briefly white, as if after all this
time we'd lost nothing across the diminishing sky.

FAITH

Husk end of August and the insects longing
for their final assignations, the high pitched
fields straining to one wire-tight note.
He's running late along the dust-skinned paths,
wind shifting in the wild laurel and eucalyptus—
dry arpeggios of the leaves, creek mumbling
from the book of water, almost a stir
of orchestral strings, but who's listening?
He's following the light flaring on the canyon's white seam—
burning sycamores, juniper, greasewood, sage,
the perfume, he thinks, of stars.

Boy with a boy's implacable heart—all that's required
from his momentary bird-like and leaping bones
to scale the sandstone crag, and on a flat rock top
find his sole response is the muted engine-
thrumming in his blood.
                            But he owns it all—
tumble weed declaiming the rusted fanfare
of sun, last inscription of pines against the long
bronze distance of the dust. Whatever moves or holds or
fades at the sky's frayed edges, accedes—hangs
balanced on the winged intercession of a cloud.

On the one hand, the impaired joy of every shining
thing he stands in perfect ignorance of—
on the other, the unlikelihood that anything
taken to heart will have the half-life of the trees.
Even the everlasting sparrows, thick in the scrub oaks,

have little to divide them from the dark, and are stopped
as if there were nothing left to be done on earth . . . .

He kicks at the clay, the foothill shale, and seashells
scruff up bleached with time like bits of broken teeth.
He turns toward the sea etching the shore with foam,
making its restitutions, its affirmations of molecule
and salt.
        The sky drifts by behind its clouds,
the trees breathe out. It all seems to rest
on some unoriginal dust slapped from his cuffs,
motes floating up howsoever on the air, suspended
a moment to sift down as sure as a mountain range.

OLD LOVE

Fall along the back road
home, 4 o'clock, and still someone's burning
corn stalks, leaves—all that past sweet for an instant
and smoldering on a gold, reconstituted haze. And the maple trees start,
streaked high as if a comet's swath cut through the tops
and set star-bursts of cadmium and bronze-red there. I know it's only a matter of time
until the colors go wind-clear, and in truth all these
sugar-sourced, irradiant leaves, like all color, like our thoughts, will work down
to a blend that's always white, a smoke that is nothing
and everything there was . . . . Even then we were on fire
beneath the immaculate lemon blossoms and stars approximate
to the north of town, electrified by the close coursings of our blood, the unbuttoning
of your white school blouse—and coming up
for air from the front seat of your parents' Chevrolet we admired
the high limbed constellations, the landscape of the dark
as a star shot by and fell white-hot with whatever dim wish our mouths then made.
Twenty five years, and I'm one of thousands now who know the intricate theories
in back of light—quantums, particles, multi-dimensional strings; I've seen the lost blue
nurseries of our stars surface on the photo plates after fifteen billion years.
But in the east each night, I watch the galaxies spin away
without a trace of us—their laundry line of dust undone but bright for all of that—
in the west, that sea-mist rising into the turquoise sky is a sentiment complete
unto itself with its salt-white, inarticulate hope . . . .
Here, there's half an hour sometimes
in an afternoon, a moment when the immolation
of the leaves calls back some light that holds me
almost breathless on a ledge
of sky before the trees die back greyly
against the cold,
and there are no stars
for this.

Orsua, Schiefen, Rosales and me
low-riding in our rebuilt '56—
we've dropped in a cam
and three duces, added
Hurst four on the floor,
Posi-Traction, slicks,
and a 4/11 rear end.
And so we can be heard
up and down State Street,
we've slapped on twice-pipes
and glass pack mufflers—
a low rumble percolating
from hood and exhaust . . .

We rib guys slicked-up on dates
in their haircuts and parents' sedans,
goose it next to them at the signal,
burning a little rubber, breaking loose
a couple quick bursts
on the crosswalks,
shouting *So's your mama,*
jacked-up as we are on nothing
better than the stupefying elixir
of our own blood
going crazy in our veins at 17 . . .

Our bronze and white Belair gleams
like milk, and we have Philosophy—
you could say we're into Aesthetics,
for we are out to look sharp
and appreciate the good for man

as it's manifest in the discrete rituals
of polish and high compression tuning,
in the introspective rhythms
of idle motoring . . .

We jive with most anyone on the street
except the Solsa brothers, their faces
rough as potatoes from all their fights.
Nor are we about to
drag for pink slips
to three blips of a flashlight
on that unfinished elbow of freeway,
or relinguish that status quo
and state of grace
in another driver's nod—
at our finger tips,
the acknowledgement,
the measured praise of peers.

We're looking out for Chuy Blanco
who cruises alone in his '57,
a Chevy so stripped of ornament,
so austere, that it's threatening
just standing still, a body
so buffed out, even air
passes it right by—so refined
that when he slows next to a theater,
you can read movie titles along the fins.
We give a little salute to Bondo
bouncing along stiffly
in his air-coiled Dodge,
and speak with something
approaching reverence
when we recall Louis de Ponce's

metallic-green Impala,
a 348 bored and stroked,
the three-speed winding
that truck engine all the way out
along East Valley Road.

Four lanes split the heart
of town—down to the beach
then back up in 2nd
trying to hit all the lights,
then a U outside Mission Paint.
Or we circle The Blue Onion,
pausing under the hot red
and royal blue neon of the sign,
sometimes backing in, ordering
cherry cokes and fries brought out
on trays and clipped to the door;
we sit up, doing our best to look
formidable and detached in white
T-shirts and Pendletons—"boss"
as someone is bound to say.

So far as we know, this is living—
rarely does anyone show up
to choose-off in the parking lot;
as rarely do we ever get
phone numbers from those girls
driving around much the same as we.
Mostly, we wheel about for hours
beneath a benevolent solar system
of light spun out from the Arlington,
State, and Granada theaters.
                    This is someplace
to be when gas is 27¢, when we're free
as the light rebounding between

the lavish chrome of bumpers—it's all gloss,
all talk, but it's everything we know
to be happy for. We have only to punch
the buttons of a radio for solutions to love,
for three minutes of unmitigated joy
or heartbreak with a beat—Roy Orbison
and the Everly Brothers, doo-wop and surf,
the Flamingos eternally asking,
"Are there stars out tonight . . .?"
This is the last time for us floating
in the sustained, slow dark, burning
in the brief firmament of our own
sweet design.
                    This was early 60s,
before anyone was making love
or money, and we thought we had a plan,
before draft notices, before we'd heard
of body bags, Napalm or Chu Lai—

                                        but all that
weightless confection of the heart
went spinning out of our lives
like music from the windows
of distant traffic, like neon
lights winking out above us
as we made a last pass
before heading home,
all of it saying, nevertheless,
that whatever we were worth,
we were worth it then . . .

DREAMING THE CLOUDS OF 1956

The tall buildings bored and sagging
against the sky—here's Woolworths,
the Granada, the Carillo Hotel, just enough
dulled gilt at the corners to keep up an air
of complacency—a bright grey burning through
the feathered palms.
         A mist moving
over the heart's long streets, fog horn
up from the breakwater like a broken vow
of happiness. A little wind reminds the eucalyptus
of something, pushes me along the sidewalks
in my haircut, my navy school sweater tied
about my waist,
         I am still the boy I remember, tugging
my mother's coat, pulling her in to the shoe store
where I stand on the fluoroscope and the green
network of my feet glows through my Buster Browns
in two clouds of mystery.
         Raindrops on the window
sparkle like stars—and later a few stars work through
clouds, blunt and silver as Coca Cola bottle caps,
a swirl and glimmering slur, river running
off in the vague direction of everything
yet to come . . .
         Long run-on sentences of rain
on the glass, and in English class, Sr. Julie told us
a preposition was anything you could do to a cloud,
though I was always somewhere between the tree tops
and the mare's-tail sky, the phrases ascending
like smoke, like chalk clapped from erasers . . .

Waylay of dust, addendum to the silt built up
in the soul's small bones—despite the scraped
knees and the unfailing numbers of pain
I counted to, nothing had undone the possibility
of the air, the pink clouds of my lungs or the harp-
like thrumming of blood along my wrists. About this sky,
nothing surrendered or doubtful as far as I could see,
as far as the world then went—boxcars, camels trailing
over the hills, the tablecloths of angels, lemon blossoms
and white caps across the bay—a horizon line
penciled in behind the floating islands . . . .

ALISOS CANYON CONTRACT

A child in the affluence
of space and leaves,
I walked out agreeing
with the trees. At my command,
the grand inheritance of the sky,
an affidavit summoned
above the sandstone and
perpetual oaks, a blank page
in back of the coastal range
on which clouds scribbled
my three initials—
proof of everything
left to me under the sun.

I hiked or rode a bike there
for the day-long business
of climbing house-size rocks,
monitoring the white
surf-curls and backwash
of indigent clouds.
                              Cars slid by
down the distant road, so many
fish shining through their deep
and watery gates. My ambition
was to gather waist-high foxtails
with my open hand. My distractions
were tangerines burning
like day-time stars in the tops
of the one foothill grove,
a buzzard tilting in his dark patrol.
No one knew me as I

knew myself in my green
and adaptable heart.
Cochise, Robin Hood, Johnny Ringo,
The Cisco Kid, I lived
those lives at once,
and no one quicker
to draw against shadows
or track the venomless lizards
to their hide-outs in stone,
to send a silver-tipped arrow
into the soft belly of a log.
Who knew better the cutoffs
and switchback paths, the crossing
rocks in pools, the free-fall stanzas
of the creek high into the hills
and all the lost Himalayas?
I believed as I was told—
anyone who wished could
have it all. The evidence
was plain as daylight
as far as I could see—
there was plenty, and plenty to share,
would always be—this was easy
as the air.
                    And as if that too
were a place you could go,
just by saying so, I stood still
in the wind and claimed
the franchise of the light
across the breathing fields.

Where did I go once
sycamores set their last star—
yellow leaves against autumn

and gave way to the grey
murmur of the boughs?
Sunset, and the yucca
and agapanthus blooms
are at a loss to say.
Here, a dull dusk covers
the day's remains, copperish
as the edge of a coin. Riffraff
of the lesser skies, sparrows
and mockers, offer up a run-down
of my immediate life and times,
the scratch in the dust
I've made, the here and now
beyond the softened margins,
the sea-colored needles
of tamarisk and pine—
the incessant breeze that just picks
at the surface of things.

◊◊◊

And if I look, as it has become
my weakness to look, for something
to correspond, to pull in to myself—
lure and sparkling spinner—
it's one star shooting lengthwise,
a nylon line cast past the surf,
a flare across the smudge pot night
that goes under with the dead
weight of hope . . . And memory
sputtering against a screen,
the early outline of that dark
for an instant or so, silvered
into smoke—spokes to a wheel
of vaporous gauze.

                    Sky with all
the house lights left on,
floating basin of the Milky Way
shifting left, footloose
in its freight, and no place
now for pity, reflexive as palm leaves
sprung into the windy night.
                                        This
is the little prayer that wakes me,
calls me back from a landscape
where trees are not cold
enough to be quiet,
has me up early with the wind,
repeating everything . . .

I want to tell myself
this is all there has to be—
sky with its citrus glaze, salt
off the spindrift stars,
an aquifer of light beyond
the old street to the sea—
and a gale off the bay,
the belled catalpa leaves
asking, Do you still want to fly?
And the green knowledge
of those sail-shaped leaves
inscribed on the evening's
parchment sheen, where
finally the blue life of air
is forfeit again into my arms.

begins with the air's lost legions—
dull as dish water clouds slumped
above the estuary, scatterings
of godwits and curlews, sanderlings
stitching the tide's white hem.

Rain recites its last novena
on the hoods of parked sedans
and a storm trundles down the coast,
dour as the old ones in their overcoats
out from Friday mass—veils and canes,
the end of afternoon that leads nowhere
beyond simmering pots and windows
steamed dim as the selfsame clouds.

But when the silk trees flower
bright as hope and suggest
the architectures of an angel's wing,
I want to be root-still, simple,
and take the next thing in the sky
as a sign of our lives spiraling
back to us, reusable as air,
as the brilliant bits of galaxies
knotted together by a dark
invisible weight,
                    which is to say
any of us turning the wind's thin page
for a hymn of light, marking our places
beyond the last thumb print of winter,

the one smudging the horizon's powder-
blue scarf, blown high up there and
snagged in a sycamore, where starlings
are grinding out something close to joy
before they reaffirm that there is
no easy grace on earth, and shatter the sky
with their faithless and frantic wings.

SINGING

I want to go back to that afternoon in my mid-twenties and
the sway-back card table pitched outside the only apartment
I could afford after finishing school. I want to unfold the legs
in the wax-green shade of the pittosporum, in the dirt that
passed for a patio there and pause to admire the ambered
southern California light as it dusts the insane orange heads
of my bird of paradise. I want a minute to encourage the three
hapless strings of ivy ascending the deathless stucco wall
from their ledge of shade—I want to see that light again braze
the metal carriage of my typewriter as the bold face hammers
away at those long legal sheets. I want to be there exactly at 3:00
when I permit myself a generous glass of Volnay, and I want that
feeling of immutability that comes with the second glass, the one
that has me rewriting the stiff title poem of that first book so
some lines loosen up and dance a little, lifting their feet enough
to make it all almost worthwhile. I want to listen and hear
the ordinary pizzicato of the 4:00 breeze and be satisfied
again with the recitative a heart gives out for any reason.

I want to be flattered for a while by the approbation of the leaves,
by the cloud-drift rhythms of my mind. I want the unqualified
good will in that third glass of wine that makes me grateful for
an afternoon without papers, leaves me so admonished by the blue
grace of evening I don't dare fear death or work, or consider parsing
the paradigms in the scattered strings of stars, the next fifteen years
going in a blur . . . If I were there, I might not bellyache about my job
and all the taxes of the state of Pennsylvania. I think I could stand
to hang around a while as I build a fire in the hibachi for chicken,
slice avocado and tomato into olive oil—a little mozzarella and bread,

my last tin of smoked oysters, thinking that young woman might
come around. And I want to be there later when I get out the only
bottle of Sandeman brandy I've ever had, pour water glasses full
and wait for the moon . . . We turn my stereo up and put on Orff's
Carmina Burana, listen to the peasants and angels praise each other
and the light of the earth, and warn about Fate until the walls of my one
miserable room quake like a tabernacle for the holy, blind joy of singing.

III

NOTE TO TOMAZ SALAMUN WHILE FLYING THROUGH A THUNDER STORM EN ROUTE TO A WRITERS' CONFERENCE

To die in the river, to die in the river.
—TOMAZ SALAMUN, from "Death's Window"

Up here, Tomaz, the clouds are not proverbs;
not the lingua franca of a vast and blue
republic of the mind—they may in fact be
the prosaic boundary stones of the world. . . .

The subject of God comes up in my knuckles
turning white, and, as you've pointed out, in *Dust*—
where it might fall, for instance. . . .
I'm thinking how close it would be

to a state of grace to be in a bright room
once more, desks facing the chalkboard
as we hear about the Tigris and Euphrates,
their fertile geography of water, their green mists

measuring and unwinding the light? Perhaps
someone showing us the fluted columns
at Persepolis, the shapes of animals in cuneiform,
or tracing-out the starry gods of Chaldea. . . .

But we're dropping through air pockets
that seem to have no air at all—and I descend
from my lofty thoughts glimpsing a slate river
crossed by shadows of angels, or dark wings?

An orange branch of lightning snaps off
beyond our wing where I've abandoned all belief
in the theoretical which tears away
from the mind as easily as this fabric

of cloud sheared by the invisible
down drafts of the cold, as easily as the linings
of cotton twine or lace-like paper doilies
we pasted around red hearts

cut out in grammar school, in February,
in another life on earth—then we spoke freely
and with confidence of love, let ourselves go
for nothing more than a phrase . . . This then

could also be History, for if I live through another
twenty minutes of my life at the merciless hand
of gravity and a wind pulling out from under us
like some magician's tablecloth,

I too will be happy just to walk to the store for milk,
to remember exactly who is who, and to praise
the unshakable faith of trees, the grains
of salt which were once the eyes of fish. . . .

ART & SCIENCE, 1961

There we were, unaccountable as the birds for air,
let go at last from a life of lessons and the school—
above us, a style of clouds I'd recognize as Constable's
20 years down the road, drifted in place and rang
against that seacoast blue like large white bells
and found an echo and equivalence in moon-
skinned peaks of the granite range, abandoned
by ocean-colored crests of digger pine and oak . . .

Clouds were inscriptions, icons, a longhand
in our own unconscious code which traced us
through the green and hillside lengths of afternoon.
We took ourselves with our arms and careful art
along the avocado boughs where we were surely
oblivious to the transmutation of the two-lane
highway widened north and south, to the impact
of boulders trucked from foothills to the sea
for a breakwater and drummed-up dredging of the bay.

Who were we then to work by induction such dark
things out, to sense anything apart from our release
to the formless rally and reprise of wind, joyous
as the surf in its renunciation of the sea? We could count
on one hand the apparent contradictions in our lives—
some to prep, some to public schools; some with money,
romance, some hurting for the same—all of which
raced out culverts of our lightly confounded hearts
as quick as riptides from the shore—all of it beyond
lasting or immediate belief, given the candles set aflame

inside in our limbs, the sunlight feeding them as we
faced the sky.

There were only those burning measures
of the light as we rode 10-speeds down Hot Springs Road,
coasting with no hands, arms spread above our heads
into the corridor between orange and olive trees, eyes
filling with the glass-bright dome, wind streaking past
our fingertips as we shouted—cirrus, cirro-cumulus,
nimbo-stratus,—every Latin name for clouds we knew,
all the science it seemed we were ever going to need.

THE SCALES—Easter, Belgrade, 1989

All week a chill grey has risen
off the Danube and the Sava
and loitered in the form of air
above the streets; a thick silence
of clouds, greyer still, hangs
like old washcloths over
the apartments and cement
architectures of the state.

And when you stand on the promontory
of Kalemegdan, the Roman fort
driven wedge-like into the convergence
of these waters, you see the flat river banks tipped
like a set of scales—new city and old,
a little played off against a little less . . .

I walk park to park to find one
free of crowds and the coal smoke
oiling the air. Only a couple dogs,
and one stray old man in overcoat and beret
shuffling along the paths; his whiskers and hair
white as chestnut spikes holding on for June.
From an oak a magpie—self-possessed
and formal in her white tie and tails—
tells a German police dog just where to get off.
Otherwise, the man is alone as anyone
I've seen. For I've watched the men
in their usual throngs wrangling over
politics or chess, smoking fearlessly,
filling the benches, strolling the great fort
all green and overgrown along the river banks,

spitting with a modicum of style
into a few managed beds of flowers.

He must have been born before
there was a Party here, even before some king.
Wife, friends all gone now—what could a holiday mean
to him, what could he be weighing out but time?
He saunters along at the contemplative rate
of clouds, in a circle around the grey edges
of the paths where no one disturbs
his memories, or where perhaps, nothing
brings them back.
                              I likewise have friends
out of reach—beyond a sea or, like his, truly beyond
some deeper blue—friends with whom I could share
a drink and make such bright recoveries in the blood
that despite the specific gravity of loss,
our dull whereabouts or the years, our home
along the coast would take us back
with sunlight down the sandstone walls,
with salt-spray skimming palms and Spanish tiles. . . .

Even so, I know it's a sin of pride to complain.
What is there finally so cloud-heavy
over the humors that the thermodynamic
mists from a Slivovitz can't burn it off,
or breathe light into it as they reach down
until the heart glows like a pearl,
a sun lifting from some far and flame-blue sea?

Nonetheless, here I am in this dark May,
and if, as Unamuno said, there is another life,
but it's shining inside the earth,
and you must keep the planks of your casket

beneath your bed to ever enter there,
we must still go to some length
to have our burdens lightened enough to see
the way clear.
           For example, this grandfather,
pacing around these pale irises
without a second thought for weather,
for his body that is now all bones
and soul—or all bones—what does he have left
except his thoughts and these flowers
against the grey, except his desire
to just keep moving?
           Children are
flitting like sparrows up and down
the pedestrian mall—the whole city
turned out on holiday, to parade
their flame-tinted hair before the unilluminated
shop windows and consumer displays.
Incense from the empty orthodox church
has drifted across the street
and found a seat at the famous bar.
Teenage girls lock arms and promenade,
soldiers smoke confidently in line
outside the theater, red and white awnings
on ice cream carts and cafes wave indifferently
in the wind.
           Just the irate magpie singing
as if there were something at stake—only
this old man taking the remaining silence on.
From where I sit, I have to think that they
are about the only ones left with a question
of heaven still hanging in the balance.

EVENING IN CORTONA

crepuscolo dalle mura
for Nadya

Along the wall at twilight, sharing the stalled summer light—
and at this height no doubt the very atoms Etruscans breathed
obscurely all that air ago—life again seems possible, continuous
as schools of salmon clouds moving south over Lago Trasimeno
or along wheat-tinted draughts of sun that fill the valley and leave
a few soul-colored wisps behind on a thinning west. . . . Eventually,
they'll grey and go to charcoal, be overtaken by the dark ebbing
between the alliteration of stars. Likewise, the heart goes
grey when it detours around the ample contentments of the day
as if there were some great seriousness behind a job which will be
there long after we have departed for an arguably lightless realm,
and after the winds, as always, have seen to all the important details
and remaining tasks. From here, you can calmly observe the train
to Rome, what might be a little afterthought of smoke laboring
slowly into nothing and the night . . .

　　　　　　　　　　　　　　　　And so, to have stepped off
at Terontola, to have removed ourselves from the commerce of the world
and the 2nd class coach, to have bought two bus tickets in the bar,
a small Cynar & lemon before taking the road's wide turns and switch-
backs to the top, was wisdom—which, is only the old wish to live
slowly and with a little satisfaction, like the potted geraniums
red in the open windows, to live in a place you choose
to plant pomegranate or loquat trees, somewhere you can stroll
among the stilled notes of afternoon and let the light find you
on a hill—this one for instance—where it won't have any trouble
picking you out on the terra-cotta path in your sun-bleached shirt
and tennis shoes, or among the water-colored junipers climbing

for the clouds.

        The wall sidewinds and braces itself against time
in all its guises of gravity and rain, against each fistful of dust
dreaming for the sea—the stones are rooted against wind, against
each wedge of absence it would place here, and stalwart, stand shoulder
to honed shoulder holding the high streets and narrow homes up.
Dusk unthreads from the last blue level of the hill; a window sends out
a single piety of light. The terraces of fig or olive saplings reveal
a breeze and afterglow, crimson on their topmost leaves, and above
the tiles and household eaves, sparrows are happy just to be getting by
where swallows bank with break-neck speed around the Piazza
della Repubblica and attest to the glorious infrastructure of the sky.

PRAYER AFTER PROMOTION

The aether must be full

of prayers too . . .

—G.B. SHAW from a letter

The trees keep reaching out for something—
light, or air, or some untrammeled space to think
their breezy thoughts, though it could be they're
just stretching after the last leptons or quarks shaken/
sparked sub-atomically from their bright branches
by the recent innuendoes and undercurrents of wind.
Of course they're just reaching for their life,
and even on the longest day of dark in December
their silhouettes betray a clustering, like galaxies—
a congregation of hands still lifted in petition there.

Clouds, the sky's lost memos—stars, in and out
of the vest pockets of the void. . . . I have a hat, and
when wind chimes start up their glass confabulations,
and plum-colored shadows stand against the house,
I walk out by the evening river where clouds and stars
repeat themselves across the surface and do not abjure—
sometimes, I tip my hat, as if my soul were also floating
there, shining as casually as the gathering dusk, as if
now I might know what I should ask to know, or like water,
or like light, be content with a modest resemblance?

One summer by the Arno, taking the evening promenade
alongside locals, we came upon a man in a raw silk coat,
a white scarf about his neck. Leaning against the wall,
lighting his pipe, he was 50 or so, comfortable and exact.
At shoulder level calmly on the wall, was a fox, obviously
a pet, with a leash and collar, with a rich red coat and great
hay-colored tail—both were smiling, and proclaiming
nothing beyond the gold window of the river, allowing
people and the world to pass, and so were untroubled
as the day drifted off and left them shining by themselves.

How lovely, even for a little while, to escape a certain
knowledge, the nota benes, the hammer-lock on the heart,
the caffeined arrhythmia at dawn. Zeno knew about career,
argued his theories of space and time long before Socrates,
tenure, or book awards: the stadium which can't be crossed
because in order to reach the end you must first reach a point
half way; before that, the point half way there, ad infinitum—
or the flying arrow occupying space; it can only be where it is
and therefore is at rest. If you cannot begin at the top, well,
you'd better become used to things around you as they are.

What would it be like to look in the mirror one day and
find two images, a lighter one turning away, breathing
easy, praising nothing more than a salt-embellished wind,
the green molecules of the sea, the atoms exchanging
their little packets of light so you can absentmindedly
whistle a patch of Puccini? But I am talking to myself
too often to simply calm down like one smooth stone
sinking slowly down a deep pool, to keep my mind, poor
constellation of dust, from spinning off, red shifted and
pulling away through unfootnoted and expanding space.

Heisenberg's Uncertainty Principle reveals that we alter,
by observing, what we observe. At the sub-microscopic
level, fluctuations in energy systems occur constantly—
in one billionth of a trillionth of a second, an electron and
its antimatter mate, the positron, can emerge out of nothing-
ness without warning, come back together again, and then
vanish. You could use up every particle of joy this quickly,
you could watch the evening news, see the bodies stacked
around the world and ask yourself, How have you risen
to the occasion of your life—What in the world have you done?

Half way to somewhere, it's probably already too late.
You might at least put down that old sack of sticks
so when the dogwood flowers with its white and immediate
suggestions, you'll be standing to one side of worry,
invisible enough to feel a principle of form spiraling
like a galaxy's recursion of nesting light. Give in then
to the pittosporum, yellow blossoms like star clusters, a thick
atmosphere of fragrance lifting you, flooding the fingers
of the dark—take in the high balustrade of eucalyptus,
a pepper-scented sea of leaves separating you from the moon.

To explain how matter and energy were conveyed across
empty space, Newton and his followers had only to attend
a meeting, but postulated instead that the cosmos was pervaded
by an unseeable substance, an Aether—an idea appropriated
from Aristotle which says essentially that there is a celestial
element of which all stars and planets are made, and which
permits them to move unimpeded—the aether wafting
right through them like wind through a grove of trees
with no aberration of starlight as we know it now—no angel
gliding steadily through bright rain, trailing her bent light.

17th century Irish theologian Bishop James Ussher—
Chairman of his department—was precise in his research
when he proclaimed that God began to forge the heavens
and earth at 2:30 on a Sunday afternoon, October 23rd 4004 B.C.
And while Einstein was sure God didn't play dice with the universe,
some ad hoc committee members questioned his methods
and supporting materials. Yet still in the laboratory
spontaneous acts of creation and annihilation have been
measured on the sub-atomic scale, neutrinos and positrons,
gravitons posited—there, and not there, at the same time.

And helpless to explain every outcome of collision, physicists
know each particle is only one possible result as nature
keeps rolling the bones, operating not as a machine but as
a game of probability. A fair chance then, we're just stitches
of light, unruly strings, four dimensional knots in a frothy
twenty-six sided glow, still listening to the fossil whisper
of the Big Bang—that red star-noise on the radio telescopes
like a long high hiss escaping from a radiator—motes more or
less advanced, but without a prayer of knowing what it means
to have come even this far, against such spirited opposition.

EARLY MORNING—Ucross, Wyoming

The hundred blackbirds lifting back
into the burning sun, into cottonwoods
and silver poplars, complain a cappella
that someone else is out beneath the sky
to appraise a portion of the green and un-
sung world, wherein some trees list
flower-like toward the bright margin of the east,
where I too find a station in the light,
quiet with my tea—
                          so all the birds come
clucking back, two-stepping from their wind-
stuttered flight and bow again to the earth
not far from where a sprinkler registers
its glistening notes across the lawn,
nor far, for that matter, from the first white-
as-paper clouds which assemble orchestrally
above the Big Horn range and mark the muted
distance off.
                   But I'm half blind before
these burnished August fields, the haze
riding the flat space out to a vanishing point
in the opened sky, and so turn to foothills
chorused on my left and right, to house shadow
and the blossomed shadows of the plums
which gradually draw back into themselves
with everything they know.
                                  Yet you begin to feel
this could save your life, this early rising
into a world the calm accompaniments of which

are grass and the sorrowless dispatch of birds,
a world in which you sit still a while
as the tender winds finger waxy willow leaves
or the damasked bells of hollyhocks ascend
their fluted stalks and call to no one, and to you.

You thought you'd had your say about the blue—
oh, the indifference, the emblem of our loss,
or those thin architectures of belief that lead us
nowhere, really, we ever wanted to be.
But here, it's all elemental each azure dawn,
composed and clear, vast and unrehearsed
as each measure of the air we take
through the wing-beats of our hearts.

THE PRESOCRATIC, SURFING, BREATHING COSMOLOGY BLUES . . . .

When the great waters went everywhere, holding the germ, and generating light,
Then there arose from them the breath of the gods.
—"Hymn to the Unknown God" from the RIG VEDA

Let's get real gone.
—ELVIS PRESLEY

The idea of an infinite number of stars brought Newton to his knees, for that would turn
the sky into a blazing haze—flame rises naturally—and so reasoned Empedocles
Homer, and Anaxagoras who filled the farthest reaches with fiery light. . . .

The back pages of cosmic history blow open, a bright litter of particles swimming in
the blue backwash of quasars, kernels back at the beginning smoldering
finally through to us now, telescopes probing not just into space
but into time. . . .

So galaxies in the Coma Cluster appear to us as they looked seven hundred million years
ago, about the time the first jellyfish—its own roseate nucleus of cells and
spinning arms—was developing on earth,

where, some years later, I would turn up at 9, walking tip toe along Miramar Beach,
avoiding the pink and scattered nebulae washed up for a mile around—
a sting like hot coals, a cold quivering mass of burning stars.

Or where I sit now, admiring a sugar maple, flag of impending flame, angelic breathing
we attribute to trees as we bivouac at the perimeter of nothing as instrumental
as beauty, and are mainly recursive, among other elemental things.

What wouldn't it be worth to have time again to worry about incursions of fog over
the blacktop, the starry orange groves dissolving on the slow drive to school,
to worry about the spelling of grey or gray, or Mississippi, the mysterious
lives of Saints, a laundry line of levitating miracles commemorated
along the church's tomb-dark walls

where beeswax candles, placed cross-wise on my throat, would save me from choking
on the bones of fish, and holy water sprinkled along the air keep a sea-wide
iniquity from seeping under the closed door of the soul so I might be
admitted to the beatific company of clouds, the clear apertures
in an updraft of wind.

And I in fact sometimes pondered the unsubstantiated Soul—invisible, but something
just the same—like a glass of water filled to different levels during music class,
sounding a high or low note as a finger orbited the transparent rim.

Or in back bookcases, The World Book Encyclopedia, all the blank space edging dark
columns of letters proclaiming the Hittites' fierce knowledge of iron, the Code
of Hammurabi, The Lighthouse at Pharos, and the first space capsule
burning like a thimble of coal in the stratosphere.

Yet, when we think about it, our youth lasts all our lives, trailing us like a comet tail of ice
and dust, or the way angels, like knots in a rope of light, are still let down to us
from the dark in Caravaggio's first "St. Matthew," the one sent up
in flames in the bombing of Berlin

whose atoms are still associated in the grey haze that constantly resettles that sky, re-
claiming its dust in the thin half-light of loss, in the past riding that freight
of light out to a universe where all things are contingent upon each other,
upon, as Anaximander had it, "The Indefinite."

There's much that matters in that dark where my hands are full of the brilliant dross
off the recent edge of discovery, data no one in school had the least idea existed
when I took my D in General Science.

Now I'm writing it all down—Vacuum Genesis, Lookback Time—thinking I'm getting
somewhere, only to realize I need another course in Italian Cinema just to
make the metaphors make sense!

Was it Luchino Visconti's *Death in Venice* or Vitorio De Sica's *Brief Vacation?* Dirk
Bogarde on the Lido coughing out the dark matter of his lungs for some
blond boy in a bathing suit as Mahler's symphony moved like a cloud
of melting glass over the sea,

or that beaten angel of a housewife escaping her truck driving, mule-headed husband
in Torino with black stars on her X-rays, a silt of light slowing in her veins
which took her up to the state sanitarium in the snowy Alps, a comet-quick
brush with a younger man reconstituting the rose-colored clouds
of her lungs, but sending her finally back?

And I remember holding my breath, the universe expanding inside my lungs as I was
tumbled like a rag in the spin-cycle of a ten foot surf a quarter mile off shore,
riding the point break at Rincon and plunged into the white salt-roar
of froth, my chest burning as I shot up to that heaven

of air above the surface—and while heaven could, in theory, have been anywhere,
it was there that minute as I swallowed the air's cool light, mindless of every
molecule and the constant state of flux all things are in.

And regardless of the frenzy of atoms and the sub-atomic voids, I'd have sold my soul
for my dinged-up plank, anything to hold to and fill my flattened pipes
before the next wave with its five feet of churning soup rolled in,
beneath which I'd have to dive, count ten, and come up again
gasping toward a low tide of rocks.

In college, staring out past the spires of Italian cypress, wind bending the invisible
    blue beyond the second story classroom windows, the thick glass sinking,
        soaked with old light, the Presocratics were proclaiming the single source
            to everything. Half conscious, at swim in the 60s, I was reaching
                for the first idea that would keep my head above dark waters.

And, like Einstein, whom I hadn't read, I didn't bother about the details and showing
    my work—all the math and elegant equations—I just wanted to know what was
        on God's mind when he shook up this boule de niege and let time-space
            float out and gather here with our little neighborhood of
                respiration and recourse to nothing but light?

But, at 19, I had recourse to little beyond beer and the bylaws of poker? Was it or
    wasn't it air? Aneximines proclaimed everything was—just rarefied and condensed—
        while Thales assured us all things were water, and I'd seen plenty of that.

They both fared better than Heraclitus who favored fire—for, the obvious consideration
    of our weight aside, as air, we were almost spirits already, and shouldn't we
        shine then at last among the aethers? Yet sinking in the specific gravity
            of over 40 years, the best I come up with most nights is moonlight
                through the trees, its mist lifting almost imperceptibly
                  through the leaves . . .

It turns out the Ionians were not that far off track; cosmic radiation—the original red hot
    atomic spin and background hum—can be tuned-in from any cold rock
        in a universe 90% back-filled with a dark and missing theoretical matter—
            that bang and microwave broadcast even the deaf still hear . . .

And so, I have little more on hand than air and a forecast of air where it is unlikely
    I'll find myself free of the old aptitude of starlight to break our hearts—though
        I look into the infinite, the nothingness, the nowhere, and the dark
            as if I recognized the light in its last disguise.

Heaven's way, lost
river of breath, this *road*
to the sky running out
along the Santa Ynez.
I'm driving the mountain crest
toward a stand of cloud-shaped trees,
one remove from the world,
the delays of light
up from the sea,
a skein of salt blistering
ironwood and manzanita.

Dragon flies cut and hum,
iridescent as gasoline, as new leaves
along the green and sunset flames.
And against the evening gloss,
jays are dark as quasars,
that deep, first-ever blue
burning through to us
after fifteen billion years—
and this is, for a moment,
a place where all the past
has gone.
                Forty years ago
my father built his tower
back here on Broadcast Peak,
and with 100,000 watts
proclaimed the power and extent
of "easy listening." He took in

76

the vista, had his vision—
the business of this world
was business, confidence
and a pressed gabardine were all
that were required for the keys
of commercial kingdoms
to fall into your hands.

And though he stood
on this promontory in the sun's
salt-haze, looked to the windward
or the lee, he was no Balboa,
and discovered little more
than men before him who embraced
the gold starred surface of the sea.
All those years he never heard
the dark ledgers thudding
shut in the small rooms
of the blood.
           But his music
is still on the air, his radio
tower pressing sentimentally
into the valley winds,
the cross-braces pitted with stars
of rust. All of it simply outlasting him
and the brief illusion
that wherever it is we are,
we spin essentially
at the center of the spheres.

But only the raptors ride up
here as thermals build, etching

cold circles in the sky, an eye
on everything humming blood-wise
in their sight. The sage, and purple
thistle, paint brush like blood flecks
vibrating on a breeze—dusk
thumbing the center of each
wind-blown bloom.

        Below, the city
shines with the emerald precisions
of pools, a pewter light glistens
off jacarandas and alexandra palms,
the Pacific stretching away
on the insubstantial promise
of the air.

        Half way back
of beyond, this is the view down
both sides of this scraggly range,
and you finally come to see
what you have come to see—
the roadside aspirating its dust,
Laguna Blanca shimmering, no more
than a mirror held up to mist.
No, this is not the end
of your life, but some days,
breathing this thin atmosphere,
only the white company of clouds,
only the sky pointing the way,
you can almost see it from here.

SYCAMORE CANYON NOCTURNE

> *But home is the form of the dream, & not the dream.*
> —LARRY LEVIS

Home again in dreams, I'm walking that foothill road
as the last morning star slips away over canyon walls—
red-gold riprap of creek rock, ferns splayed in the blue
shade of oaks, the high yellow sycamores, oat straw catching
sun at my feet. Wind-switch, then the chalk-thick stillness
saying *angels,* who come down here to dip their wings
and give the water its color.
                Yet even when I'm allowed back
along the weedy path of sleep to this green and singing space,
I know someday air will be set between my shoulder blades
and arms and all my bones, and, little more than clouds,
the clouds will be my final lesson until I'm taken off
into some clearer imagining . . .
              In exile, it is hard to love God.
What then, must I renounce? The Psalter of evergreens
ringing along Sheffield drive? The loquat and acacia
burning through ocean fog? Can I speak of love
almost a life ago, syllables repeating the skin's sweet salts
and oils like lemon blossoms riding the August heat?

I love the life slowly taken from me, so obviously spun out
flower-like, and for my own use, it seems, against some future
sky—the world, just a small glory of dust above a field
one autumn afternoon—the resinous pines and a back road
full of birds inside you.

What more could wishes be,
who would live there again, sent back among the breathing
acanthus to lift unconsciously with morning and with mist?
I would.

Moonlight or dreamlight, this is the world, giving
and taking away with the same unseen hand, desires winding
around the soul like fleshy rings on a tree. Where this canyon
levels out, I'd eat the wild sun-red plums, the sweet light
of the juice carrying through me my only hymn.

I know God, old flame wearing through the damp sponge
of the heart, that candle I cannot put out coming back
each time it seems extinguished. And so I must bless everything,
take anything given me—these words, their polish or pity,
the absences they bear like winter trees ascending
the ridge, so many starving angels in the early dusk,
and then the dark, and the broken order of prayer. . . .

I know you are listening. Like the sky. And the birds
going over, aren't they always full of light? But to shine
like these trees again, that air hovering on the canyon walls—
sometimes, all I want to be is the dreaming world.